hybrid INTERIORS

hybrid INTERIORS

NEW COMBINATIONS FOR
CONTEMPORARY LIVING

FRANCESO ALBERTI and **DARIA RICCHI**
principal photography by **MARIO CIAMPI**

Thames & Hudson

Essays by Francesco Alberti and Daria Ricci
Translated from the Italian by Rebecca Milner

All photographs by Mario Ciampi except for the photographs on
pages 55–61, 136–143 and 247–257 which are by Alessandro Ciampi

First published in the United Kingdom in 2007 by
Thames & Hudson Ltd, 181A High Holborn,
London WC1V 7QX

www.thamesandhudson.com

British Library Cataloguing-in-Publication Data
A catalogue record for this book is available from the British Library

ISBN: 978-0-500-51388-0

Printed and bound in China

CONTENTS

♦ Extraordinary—Familiar
☀ Home—Work
🌿 Interior—Exterior
▦ Historic—Contemporary

INTRODUCTION

Why is a nineteenth-century Indian bed being used as a table? Why have chairs fashioned out of elk horns been placed in a room with hand-decorated walls in a historic Tuscan building? Why is there a hydromassage bathtub in the center of a dinner table surrounded by work stools? The answer, which may upset purists, lies in a simple given: interior design is ruled only by what is possible. That is to say, within the field of applied creativity there are effective paths to paradox, routes that go a long way toward finding a place for new aesthetic combinations.

Domestic interiors are fertile territory for pioneering experiments with images from the past, present, and future. They are laboratories where categories, cultures, purposes, places, and lifestyles are mixed and matched. The resulting spaces—be they the fruit of a formulated design or of a process of accumulation diluted by time—have a common trait: they are all "hybrid." They play the game of the opposites to express different paths and processes: the search for the "zen" of a higher equilibrium, the pursuit of pure visual or poetic effect, ironic interpretations of ordinary spaces in a Dada or pop key, or the ideological provocation manifested by heretical combinations of form, color, and function.

Hybrid Interiors presents twenty-five spaces that show a rich variety of situations and contexts—from Amsterdam to Rome, and Berlin to Beijing—that demonstrate the studied dialectic between contemporary design and pre-existing structures, between domestic functions and working space, between materials and forms, and between classic style and popular culture.

Four different interpretations of "hybrid" accompany the reader along this intentionally erratic journey, comparing interiors that express, often through very different mediums, a similar interplay of opposites. Homes where daily life is colored by unusual objects and settings are found under the heading *Extraordinary-Familiar*; *Home-Work* houses the evermore fashionable trend of overlapping private and working areas; *Interior-Exterior* brings down the boundaries of domestic walls to merge the dwelling in the surrounding landscape; finally, *Contemporary-Historic* summarizes periods and styles in a crossover of eras where signs of the past meet the present. These four interpretations pursue one another and become mixed within the book, becoming in turn "hybridized" allowing variable and personal interpretations and offering readers moments of inspiration and ideas for their own homes.

BETWEEN
PUNK
AND DECO
—*Berlin*

Opposite: A large dining table with a Jacuzzi tub, the seats placed around it are telescopic work stools. The iron candelabra is by the Hamburg designer Torsten Neeland. The golden lamé curtains serve as partitions and drapes for the windows.

In Kreuzberg, the most "in" of Berlin's "out" areas, two floors of an old manufacturing building host atelier Cocktail, specialized in metal and ceramic art objects, and the home of one of its founders, designer Heike Mülhaus. The interior design of these renovated spaces express two complementary sides of its owner's personality, entrepreneur and creative.

The open working space is simply and rationally organized. Modular metal frames have been assembled to form tables, containers, and trolleys, arranged in an orderly fashion as required by the cycle of production. At the same time, the loft is animated by a theatrical style and an unconventional spirit revealing Heike Mülhaus's passion for the "philosophy" and aesthetic of punk (and her capacity as a designer). The large rectangular room maintains the characteristics of the original shell. Ducts and tubes, belonging to mechanical systems, cover the walls and have been kept strictly on view as have the iron support beams. There are no fixed partitions to interrupt the continuity of the space, which is emphasized by the choice of a single industrial floor covering. Gilded lamé curtains run in front of the windows and across the room acting as dividers and as theater curtains for the "inventions" that characterize the different areas of the house. Among these creations is a monumental masonry bed, clad in black majolica beneath a canopy of the same color, which brings to mind, with a certain dark irony, the vampire-like settings from cult B-movies.

The chief attraction of all the furnishing is in the living area: a large square table

with three chairs each side, made from rough industrial materials that contrast with the smooth ceramic surface of an immense circular Jacuzzi set as the centerpiece. The eccentricity of a hedonist? The ambiguity of a voyeur? Provocation against the conventions of the bourgeoisie lifestyle? Or simply the experimentation of new juxtapositions in homage to a paradoxical aesthetic? Perhaps all these things together, enriched by another cinematographic reference, this time in relation to a cultured master like Louis Buñuel and the scenography of Pierre Guffroy in their *Le fantôme de la liberté* (*The Phantom of Liberty*).

Objects created by other "extreme" designers of the German school, scattered around the loft with scenographic flavor, help to intensify the surreal atmosphere, such as the Cologne Pentagon group's Dada inspired *lounger*, or Hamburg designer Torsten Neeland's immense candelabra watching over the Jacuzzi (an exhibit, it could be said, from the tools owned by Dr. Caligaris, a character from a German expressionist film). In addition to these are the ceramic works and decorations created by Mülhaus herself, whose shapes and colors go some way to softening the "hard" overall character: screens, braziers, candelabras, and pedestals recalling the shapes and motifs of art deco are the only evidence of a tradition—that thousand-year-old tradition of terracotta and artisan work—present in this metropolitan interior.

Above: Behind a golden curtain is another of Heike Mülhaus's scenographic inventions: a black ceramic four-poster bed. In the foreground a brazier produced by Cocktail sits next to a Dada inspired *lounger*, created by the Pentagon group from Cologne.

Opposite: A small lawn has grown in a corner of the studio; some of the owner's creations are alongside.

Opposite and right: A rank
of braziers marks the doorway
from the studio to the living
area where a ceramic mosaic
screen mounted on wheels and
a vase and plate composition
on a rustic table can be found.

Left: A wide variety of
materials and colors
characterize the objects
manufactured by Cocktail,
which cheer up different
corners of the loft.
Opposite: All the mechanicals
have been left in sight. The
screen is a mosaic of pieces
of ceramic.

Opposite: A sink and an old-style bathtub are the only fixtures in the bathroom where all of the plumbing is exposed. Only curtains separate the bathroom area from the rest of the loft. The patterns of the fabrics, together with the colorful ceramic objects, give the small room a distinctive playfulness.

Above: View of the Cocktail atelier workrooms.

ART AND RECYCLING
—Berlin

Opposite: A detail of the bedroom reveals pieces of furniture created by recycling discarded materials. A painting by the owner of the residence sits among the plants. The small red table is part of the *Meridian* series by Bruno Brunati and Carlo Zerbaro for Cidue.

Overleaf, left: In the studio is *Chandelier-Boulder* by Herbert Jakob Weinand for Design Galerie, made with polyester and halogen spotlights; feminine figures painted by Elvira Bach hang on the walls.

Overleaf, right: In the sitting room are sofas of Swedish origin, a rug by Elvira Bach, and *Chandelier-Rocket* by Herbert Jakob Weinand.

Elvira Bach is one of the few members of the artist group of Jungen Wilden, which animated East Berlin art scene in the late seventies and early eighties, who managed to gain international fame. Known for depicting women's bodies (often her own) with bright colors and naive style, she was particularly fond of painting primordial figures of Eve entwined by serpents and with the forbidden fruit in hand. A few paintings from this period of her career color the walls of her home. Elvira Bach lives in a prestigious apartment building in a central Berlin. The tall luminous interiors have old-fashioned detailing including ornamental coffered ceilings. The furniture on the other hand is contemporary, perhaps a bit out of fashion but not overly so. The refined recycling of objects—a trash can supported tabletop, found chairs—are the fruit of the artist's imagination. A few carefully chosen design objects, such as a fifties *Cone Chair* by Verner Panton and a rug that reproduces one of Bach's paintings, round out the studied spaces of this apartment.

EASY CHIC
—Berlin

Above: The anodized aluminum *Palla*, designed by Herbert Jakob Weinand, is coupled with the classically decorated stucco ceiling.

Opposite: A doorway decorated with a mosaic of diverse ceramics, a work by the atelier Cocktail, marks the entrance to the study. On the floor and ceiling, the spherical lighting fixtures placed on the floor, and the chandelier were all designed by the owner.

In 1985 Design Galerie opened on Berlin's Wielandstrasse. It was a hotbed of art and design, and a place where the most creative and intriguing figures—artists, designers, artisans—of the time met. The owner, Herbert Jakob Weinand, a designer himself, lives in an apartment a short distance from the gallery. His home has a classic Berlin style interior, with majestic rooms, soaring glass windows, fine stuccowork, and herring bone patterned parquet flooring.

The furnishings are curious and eccentric. Some of the objects are handmade, one-off pieces or prototypes perhaps destined to be produced in limited editions. A stainless steel chandelier, in the form of a spherical UFO with lighted spikes, meets the classic stuccowork ceiling of a bourgeoisie apartment; a portrait of a cow greets whoever sits at a table balanced on tree trunks—all the furnishings and objects, between art and craft, are keys to the original lifestyle not only of the person who acquires them, but also of the person who invents and uses them.

Opposite: In the study
the stark materials of the
bookshelf, a concrete beam
with wooden shelves, contrasts
with a classic piece, the *Ball
Chair* by Eero Aarnio.
Right: The painting of a cow
is by Bernd Zimmer. The
table with wooden legs and
a concrete top is a Jenz Peter
Schmidt design for Design
Galerie. The rolling chair is of
American origin while the stool
in the foreground and the steel
cabinet on wheels are pieces
designed by the owner. The
Snoopy lamp on the table is
by Achille and Pier Giacomo
Castiglioni for Flos.

THE DISCREET CHARM OF THE BOURGEOISIE
—*Milan*

Opposite: The French door in the kitchen opens onto a balcony that faces the interior of the structure. The wooden cabinets on the right are part of the *Colombo* collection by Cappellini International Interiors; woven *Paola* chairs by Ferruccio Laviani for Ismet are placed around a table by Mondo. The chandelier dates back to the beginning of the twentieth century.

With exquisite negligence a Francis Bacon painting is placed on a radiator, other paintings lean against the walls. Little details like books and sculptures sitting on chairs, jars of shells, and driftwood on a bookshelf, seem to have been brought together in a casual manner, chosen with nonchalance. This Milanese interior collects influences from all over the world. It is difficult to speak of one style, or identify different styles, but the common thread is an awareness that each element reveals a glimpse of the passion and deep knowledge of the best design.

The traditional constituents of interiors are placed like exotic conversation pieces, such as the nineteenth-century four-poster bed and the cast-iron tables in the living room. Putting a bed in the living room is certainly a re-interpretation of traditional norms, yet the piece fits perfectly into the atmosphere of the home that includes a number of contemporary designer pieces. The result is a dwelling that is able to transform itself in accordance with its residents; a timeless space that can be changed and adapted to new needs.

The residence was created by renovating and joining two small apartments. The work radically transformed the features of the two previous dwellings with the demolition of the internal partitions. The original flooring, with the exception of the entrance hall, was replaced with darkened and polished planks of pine. The walls are covered with rough plaster mixed with powdered colors that differ from room to room.

The restoration work did not spoil the reserved charm of the apartment; decorative fittings along the edges of the ceilings, windows, and floors were restored and rendered more visible. Each room is elegantly furnished with a collection of furniture gradually assembled after numerous visits to markets and antique shops.

Soft lighting and warm fabrics create a warm and comforting atmosphere in the apartment. The smaller rooms and hallways induce contemplation, while the larger rooms offer exotic settings to entertain company. There is plenty of space; there are no crowded corners in this window-rich light filled residence—sunlight being the ultimate luxury in the heart of the city.

Left: The large light-filled living room was created by tearing down walls of the two apartments that now make up one residence. The dark, wax polished pine board flooring and colored plasterwork walls give the space a rustic flavor. The armchair and camp bed in the foreground, and the pair of small cast iron tables, all date back to the nineteenth century. The gold colored table is by Meret Oppenheim for Simon Interieur. The paper lamp is a classic piece by Isamu Noguchi. In the background the two Cuba sofas are by Dordoni for Cappellini.

Overleaf, left: In the living room, a *Samir* table, with a decorative wooden pattern, stands in the foreground on the left. A work by Luisa Cevese made of silk tie remnants accompanies a four-poster bed. A radiator hosts a painting by Francis Bacon.

Overleaf, right: A view of the living room looking toward the dining room, in the evening.

Right: A view of the dining room at night, classic chairs by Arne Jacobsen for Fritz Hansen flank a glass table. Two Baccarat crystal candelabras and a pair of Indian silver goblets from the eighteenth century sit on the table. On the right is a painting by Angelo Micheli, on the left a Mondo stand, and in the background a table created from a vase stand with the *Lumière* lamp by Dordoni for Foscarini.

Left: A shiny vessel designed by Ferruccio Laviani for First Folio, an art deco stand, and a vase by Giò Ponti produced by the manufacturer Richard Ginori sit on a console table in the Empire style from the fifties. The painting above the table is by Maurizio Fracassi.
Opposite: The entrance hall, with its original flooring, has a pair of chairs from the *Home* collection of Ferlea and an antique torch holder transformed into a lamp. Next to the window is a printed Abet laminate covered column with a silver vase produced by Morandotti on Ferruccio Laviani's design, and a wood and cloth screen found in an antiques market.

Previous pages, left: The guest bedroom is furnished with a *Mandarin* bed by Imel, a table-lamp in Murano glass designed by Daniela Puppa and Franco Raggi, and a small custom-made bookcase. A *Mondo* armchair, *Samir* table and *Orione* lamp by Dordoni for Artemide sit in the foreground and a mat rug from Tunisia lies on the floor.

Previous pages, right: On top of a custom-made bookcase in the guest bedroom are a print from the nineteenth century and a flagpole finial.

Left and above: Two views of the master bedroom. On the left are two layers of curtains that conceal a closet with mirrored doors. On the floor near the window is a collection of wooden forms for making hats. The vase on the table is from the *100% Make Up* collection coordinated by Alessandro Mendini for Alessi, and the chairs are *Blue-Red* by Rietveld.

Overleaf: A pair of doorways in the master bedroom lead to the hallway and a bathroom. The wooden chairs date to the early twentieth century and the painting to the late seventeenth century. In this photograph, Grazia Montesi and Raimondo Garau's precious fabric from the seventeenth century covers the bed. A *Taccia* lamp produced by Flos and designed by Achille and Pier Giacomo Castiglioni stands on a cast-iron bedside table from the nineteenth century. A glimpse of a wooden towel rack in the bathroom can be seen through the doorway on the left.

Above and opposite: The French door that opens onto a small terrace gives the bathroom a light and spacious atmosphere. The red walls and the decor are openly inspired by Pompeian motifs. The large Empire style mirror is countered with rationalist pieces (on the right is a stool designed by Le Corbusier for Cassina) and a spartan lighting system. The wicker armchair is produced by Mondo.

THE HOUSE AS A SET
—Amsterdam

Rob Eckhardt has turned his gallery into one of the most important addresses in Amsterdam for those interested in discovering new trends in furnishings. Greatly diverging from the functional roots of classic Dutch design, he has made his gallery into a stage for ideas; a place where furnishing objects are released from the utilitarian role they are usually assigned, and where their sculptural qualities are acknowledged and valued.

An eloquent example of the interior styles advocated by Eckhardt can be found a short distance from his gallery, on the top floor of a building that faces one of the old city's canals—in one of the most coveted residential areas in Amsterdam—renovated by Eckhardt with his colleague Goos Leeuwenstein. The first stage of the architectural intervention was the demolition of all the internal walls. In this way the cramped rooms of the pre-existing structure—that were used as school rooms and offices—became a single room, unusually large for this part of the city, with an annex to be used as a dining area located beyond a sliding glass door. The sleeping area occupies a mansard and is connected to the living room by a new spiral staircase.

These recaptured spaces have benefited from the participation of young artists and designers called upon to create ad hoc works and adapt their creations to the renovated interiors. The owner of the apartment, Inger Kolff, was also involved in this design *charrette*. She was able to implement her professional talents as a supervisor of photographic sets in her own home.

Beyond the succession of windows overlooking the canal, the outlines of old buildings create a backdrop against which sofas and storage units, screens and decorative objects, and paintings and flower arrangements stand out against the Oregon-pine boards in the living room. The contrast derived is visually and emotionally evocative: outside, the stable image of the historic city, framed by soft fuchsia curtains; inside, a variable and imaginative contemporary lifestyle, always searching for new forms and a language with which to express its continuous transformation.

Previous pages: The large living room was created by tearing down all the pre-existing internal walls. The space is defined by strongly characterized surfaces: the Oregon-pine floor, the sequence of windows and drapes, and the background wall painted by two young artists, Bart Gorte and Leo van Veldhuizen. Other pictorial marks help to create a rarefied atmosphere, like a photographic set: Josephine Colson's screen and the *Are You Angry, Get a Rose* rug by Maarten Vrolyk (from Rob Eckhardt's design gallery).

Above: A conversation corner with a *Lota* sofa by Eileen Gray for Vereinigte Werkstätten, and Franco Raggi's *Elbalunga* chaise-longue produced by Cappellini International Interiors. The small tables are series complements from the fifties.

Opposite: One of the two jellyfish-like sculpture-objects standing in the corner near the window is actually a small secretaire with a folding door and drawers (from the *Fruits de mer* series by Miriam van Kuppenweld).

Above: One wall of the living room is almost entirely occupied by French doors (which are also framed by drapes suspended on metal rods) that lead to the kitchen and to the dining area. The kitchen is separated from the dining area by a wood partition, realized with pieces from two different Boffi collections, that matches the color of the flooring.

Opposite: A view of the dining room. The table, with a red walnut top, was custom-designed by Goos Leeuwenstein; placed around the table are *Costes* chairs designed by Philippe Stark and produced by Aleph. Two references to the Far East complete the furnishing: a "vintage" portrait of the last empress and a *Butterfly* lamp by Afra and Tobia Scarpa.

Above, left: The span of lilac drapes continues along the wall facing the internal courtyard. Lacquered panels in the same color enclose the landing of the elegant spiral staircase with its wide Oregon-pine steps that lead to the mansard.

Below, left: One of the lacquered divider doors that articulate the mansard space (and that are also reflected in the mirror in the background) opens onto the bathroom, which is lit by a skylight. The furnishing is basic and "technological" with a hint of imagination: the water pipes below the sink wind around the steel risers that hold a mirror and shelves.

Opposite: In a corner of the cooking area, a row of tulips placed in small Campari bottles decorates the window that faces the internal area of the city block.

MEDITERRANEO
FIORENTINO
—*Florence*

It is surprising to find a dwelling in the center of historic Florence, a city known for its Renaissance architecture, that has an interior dominated by Mediterranean and Middle Eastern motifs. The apartment, in a small early-twentieth-century building in Oltrarno, accommodates a sophisticated juxtaposition of objects, colors, and furnishings creating a unique environment that reflects the creative spirit of the owners.

Throughout the space there are coherent ensembles seemingly detached of elements united by colorful backgrounds. The clean basic tones have been placed to create contrasts. In the bathroom deep shades of blue and cyclamen pink evoke the relaxing and convivial atmosphere of a Turkish bath. One corner of the room is occupied by the bathtub which is set in a masonry structure with rounded ornamentations and decorative tiles. Another corner of the bathroom has white sofas with multicolored cushions and a small wicker table with a blue glass Moroccan tea service.

The pale blue walls of the kitchen are framed by a sunny orange tone of the entry. Furnished with a simple wooden table and wicker padded chairs, the kitchen seems to belong in a country house rather than a city apartment. The owners chose to insert a metal lamp into this setting, mixing in an element with a more contemporary style. The kitchen leads to an internal garden/living room where natural sunlight filters through the city windows. A small loft space takes advantage of the full height of this central room. The distinctive atmosphere of the room, suffused with peace and privacy, makes it the perfect place to reflect and create.

Mediterranean and Middle Eastern influences are found throughout the apartment; the geometric lines of the decorative elements, ceramic adornments, multicolored carpets, and bright colors all speak of the owners' passion for the East. The majestic crystal chandelier in the central room, bringing to mind Venetian glass-blowers and aristocratic court balls in Louis XIV's France, is surprisingly harmonious with the Eastern motifs that envelop the apartment. A touch of high society Europe in this Eastern flavored residence located in the shadow of Michelangelo's David.

Right: There are very few doors in the apartment making the rooms seem larger than they actually are. The oriental rugs, bright colors, and geometric forms in this Florentine residence are all evocative of the Middle East.

Previous pages, left: The living room has warm yellow tones and is furnished with numerous Moroccan rugs; it lacks chairs and tables.

Previous pages, right: The furnishing of the bedroom is very simple, with the exception of the canopy bed.

Above and opposite: The bathroom is also a sitting room; a bathtub and low sofas share the space; arched designs have been cut into the masonry structure that holds the bathtub.

HALLS OF ART
—*Rome*

Above: The painting in the entry is a portrait of Giuliano Briganti and Luisa Laureati, *The Secret of Eternal Youth*, by Mario Schifano.

Opposite: Sebastian Matta's *Trans-aparence* hangs on the right wall, and Franco Angeli and Pino Pascali's *U.S.A. Armysull* is high up on the left wall. The sculpture in the center, *Open-air Sculpture* is by Tano Festa.

During the forty years they ran the Gallery dell'Oca in Rome, Luisa Laureati and Giuliano Briganti assembled a varied collection of eclectic and refined furniture, objects, and works of art. In addition to this collection of modern and antique works they also put together a vast library of precious volumes. In a move that is perhaps a bit unusual in the Eternal city (and more common in New York, London or Paris) the gallerists transferred their private collection to a spacious residence on the top floor of a building.

Luisa Laureati energetically transfigured part of the large apartment in the center of Rome into a contemporary gallery with dove-gray smoothed concrete floors. The enormous high-ceilinged rooms are connected by a series of beautiful gold-edged doorways that lead from one to the other. These renovated spaces are immersed in a shadowy, bookish atmosphere this is often found in the homes and private galleries of great connoisseurs. The immense collection of books is housed in a two-level library with an iron catwalk. Works by Morandi, Picasso, De Pisis, Boeckling, Maratta, Allori, Carracci, Appiani, Vernet, Kounellis, Paolini, Ontani, Mattiacci and Nunzio, to name but a few of the artists, are tastefully placed alongside neoclassical and neo-Gothic pieces.

In Bernini's Rome the windows in these spaces would have commanded magnificent Borromean views. Today the light that enters these windows illuminates Arte Povera and sophisticated installations of conceptual art. The intelligent placement of the various artworks creates the impression that they are having a conversation.

Above: In one of the galleries, *Dust* by Giulio Paolini rests on a Plexiglass surface; Jannis Kounellis' *Untitled* is next to the window; hanging on the wall on the left is *Sun Moon* by Eliseo Mattiacci.

Opposite: The two-story library was designed by Stefano Stefani and Luca Leonori; the sculpture hanging above the table is *Magnetic Time* by Eliseo Mattiacci.

Overleaf: In the living room the gold armchair is by Sebastian Matta; behind the cast terracotta bust by Arturo Martini is the painting *Towards the Temple of Bacchus* is by Arnold Böcklin.

Opposite: On the wall on the left is a photograph by Mimmo Jodice, *Cuma*; above the door hangs a work in brass, copper, fabric, plaster, and tempera on wood by Fausto Melotti.

Right: Above an adjacent golden door frame is another work by Fausto Melotti.

Overleaf, left: A smaller space houses works by Giulio Paolini (hanging on the wall to the left of the window) and Claudio Parmiggiani (the violin case to the right of the window).

Overleaf, right: Above the chair is painting by Alfred Stevens titled *Etretat*.

Left: A copper pan and bread knives harmonize with the works of art; the etching *Variations* is by Alberto Burri.
Opposite: Hanging on the wall of the dining area is a Korean work from the late eighteenth century.
Overleaf, left: The lounger is made of briarwood. *You Speak Too* by Claudio Parmiggiani sits in the Plexiglass case. On the wall are full figure portraits of men of the Demidoff family by Auguste Raffet.
Overleaf, right: Another work by Claudio Parmiggiani hangs above the bed in the bedroom. At the foot of the bed is Marcel Breuer's *Wassily* chair.

Opposite: The large painting in the background, *Emblematic Violet,* is by Giulio Turcato. The ceramic piece by the window, *Chair, Coat, Hat,* is by Leoncillo.

Above: The gold plated iron bed in the guest room is from the eighteenth century. The large painting, *Outside the Image*, above the bed is by Sebastian Matta. On the wall on the left is a painting by Giulio Turcato; small drawings by Sebastian Matta, Giulio Paolini, and Alighiero Boetti sit on top of the bookcase.

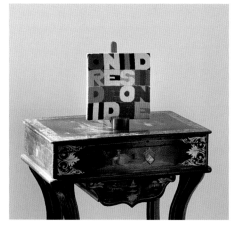

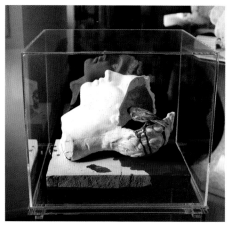

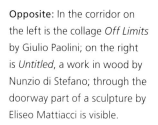

First row: Alighiero Boetti, *Order and Disorder*; Eliseo Mattiacci, *time is a friend to me, space is essential to me*; Claudio Parmiggiani, *You Speak Too*.

Second row: Filippo de Pisis's painting, *Demolitions in Milan*, Luigi Ontani's sculpture, *Christopher Columbus*; Claudio Parmiggiani, *Untitled*; Claudio Parmiggiani, *Chalice*.

Third row: Giorgio Morandi's painting, *Still Life* and Arturo Martini's sculpture *Giuditta*; Eliseo Mattiacci, *Circular Sculpture: Cosmic Order*; Claudio Parmiggiani, *Untitled*.

Opposite: In the corridor on the left is the collage *Off Limits* by Giulio Paolini; on the right is *Untitled*, a work in wood by Nunzio di Stefano; through the doorway part of a sculpture by Eliseo Mattiacci is visible.

IMPULSE AND RIGOR
—*Lucca*

Opposite: The interruption of a wooden floor and the insertion of a glass screen allow the space used as a kitchen to be separated from the double-height hallway that, via a spiral staircase, leads to the truncated floor above.
Overleaf, left: The "rocaille" style is revived in these vases encrusted with shells from the nineteenth century. On the walls, traditional garlands interweave with stylized flowers; overlapping decorations belonging to different eras and styles brought to light by the restoration work.
Overleaf, right: A low table-sculpture and two armchairs with elk horn frames also inhabit the living room.

The restoration carried out by architect Gabriella Carmassi inside a building on the historic Via Fillungo in Lucca, brings the original structure of the building back into view. The once spacious dimensions of the rooms located in the oldest part of the edifice have been recovered by tearing down internal partitions inserted by previous restorations. The creation of a new system of vertical connections restores the continuity of external walkways, reopening the three floors of stairs and the balconies that faced the courtyard.

The passage of time has been carefully highlighted by the restoration work; for example the removal of the plaster has exposed irregularities in the structure of the brickwork, revealing modifications made to the building over the centuries. This apparently neutral attitude with respect to the past (no historical era is privileged at the expense of others) reveals its "creative" nature to the full when applied to the internal finishing and decoration. In particular, the choice to preserve and clean extensive "samples" of wall and floor decoration belonging to different styles and movements, within a single room, produces a completely unexpected patchwork-effect.

This layering of the past is clearly superimposed with signs of the present, dictated more by an altered sensibility to the space, not by the requirements of contemporary life. In this restoration the contemporary insertions are softened by the shapes and materials selected by the architect—the new exterior and interior fixtures in wood and brass, the slim metal spiral staircase introduced into the double-height hallway (created by cutting into a wooden floor), and the sleek custom-made furnishings in the kitchen.

The furnishing introduces a "Dionysian" element to the space. Bizarre antiques from the city's numerous antique galleries (Lucca enjoys international notoriety in the field of antiques) burst into the rooms together with creations by contemporary artists and designers "touched" in various ways by a baroque aesthetic. Unusual materials and strange shapes, for the most part natural or at least inspired by nature, creep into the spaces between the classic antique and modern furniture: vases encrusted with shells, chairs made of elk antlers, and sculptures and paintings that reproduce stylized vegetable forms. Next to the English fireplaces, writing desks, and neoclassical vases, these peculiar pieces transform the "quiet rooms" of this antique palazzo into a surprising curiosity cabinet.

Previous pages, left: The
iron and rubber *Vines* resting
against the wall in the corner
of the living room wall is a
creation by Vittorio Corsini,
as is the small crystal tree
on the cherrywood console
table visible through the
doorway, above which hangs a
silhouette made of fabric and
buttons.

Previous pages right: The
interplay of the layers of
decorative backgrounds is
visible in this corner of the
living room.

Left and opposite: The
painting *Impressions of
Acacie* by Massimo Birzaghi
stands out against the layered
background. The room is
enriched by the addition of
furnishing objects that are
expressions of different periods
and tastes: the cushioned
stools in nineteenth-century
Regency style, the neo-
Liberty style chairs, the floral
sculptures by Vittorio Corsini,
and the iron and rubber
Water Lilies placed on the
floor (opposite), and the glass
and metal *Flower Box* leaning
against the wall (left).

Previous pages, left: The floral bands and painted frames on the walls, together with the terracotta floor, belong to the history of the building. The furnishings—different interpretations of contemporary, like the simple cherrywood tables coupled with rustic chairs and objects of art—stand out against this layered background. The painting on the wall is by Massimo Birzaghi; the floral sculpture on the floor is by Vittorio Corsini.

Previous pages, right: A detail of a door "disguised" by the wall decorations.

Left: A view of the living room from one of the terraces in the building's courtyard. There is a noticeable contrast between the sobriety of the architectural language (exposed brickwork and simple window and door frames) and the expressive power of the furnishing.

Opposite: The residence has three levels that encircle a courtyard. The various floors of the dwelling are connected by external staircases and terraces and by stairs in the interior of the building.

WRITTEN IN STONE
—*Pisa*

Above: This building in Pisa is an important example of a Pisan tower-house. The history of the structure can be discerned from the patterns of overlapping stones on the exterior.

Opposite: View of the entrance to the apartment from the external landing. Following a spare aesthetic, the entry is without furnishings.

Overleaf, left: A wood and brass framed glass wall creates an interior terrace or greenhouse that encloses a young tree.

Overleaf, right: View of the living room and interior terrace on the top floor. A stone staircase connects all three floors of the residence.

Once described as the "city of one hundred churches" Pisa has numerous examples of medieval architecture. Among them is a building that dates back to the eleventh century renovated by architects Gabriella and Massimo Carmassi, leaving the passage of time visible. The building, in the heart of this small Tuscan town, is characterized by its exterior, particularly the side facing the street; the progressive overlapping and juxtapositioning of the pilasters, stone beams, brick infilling, and rectangular windows added and subtracted over the course of the centuries are all visible in the face of the building.

The dimensions of the load-bearing walls allowed considerable internal restoration work to be carried out during the eighteenth century. These interventions caused the original spacious layout of the structure, which was without partitions, to be lost in favor of an inflexible divided space. Nevertheless the architects decided not to try to go back to the ancient layout (which would also be difficult to define with precision), and instead chose to adapt the existing spaces to create a home and offices for their clients. A previous renovation subdivided the building into apartments, one on each floor. Now, after the most recent renovation, the second floor hosts offices, bedrooms are on the third floor, and a central internal stone staircase leads to the top floor where the kitchen and living room are located.

Some of the dividing walls on the top floor have been removed, emphasizing the old exquisite wooden trusses in the ceiling. An abundance of sunlight enters through large arched windows with a marvelous view of the city. The plan to open more arched windows along the façade facing the street was not feasible, so the opportunity to have a terrace was lost. Plaster does not easily adhere to stone, consequently all the plaster was removed from the external walls of the building. Plaster was also entirely removed from internal walls where there were strong pre-existing decorative elements, which were then restored and enhanced. In other areas of the interior, irregular gaps in the plasterwork reveal sections of ancient masonry walls. This delightful "dilapidated" style acquires a contemporary feel through the presence of fixtures and furnishings with modern designs and materials. Another example of mixing existing and modern designs is the series of glass panels that defines a small internal terrace. This small "greenhouse" is located in front of an eighteenth-century arched window, liberated from an infill of bricks, that is without any glass or shutters.

Opposite: In the dining area of the living room antique chairs surround a glass table. An irregular section of the old wall was left exposed after the restoration work. The kitchen is visible through the doorway on the right.

Right: Here the restoration work exposed an attractive double-arched architectural feature in the wall. The iron window frame is set back in such a way that it forms a second aperture of glass.

Overleaf, left: View of the study with glimpses of a *Nuvola Rossa* bookcase by Vico Magistretti for Cassina, a table by Le Corbusier, and a lamp by Ettore Sottsass.

Overleaf, right: The *Nuvola Rossa* bookcase contains hundreds of Mickey Mouse comic books. The contrast between the exposed-brick wall and the old plasterwork decoration is evident.

Left and opposite: Two rooms after the restoration work was completed; signs of the passing of time have been left unaltered. Long forgotten decorations and a fireplace are in full view.

ESSENTIAL
AND PRECIOUS
—*Vienna*

Right: The dining area of Delugan & Meissl's *Ray I*. The walls of windows and the absence of opaque partitions create the feeling of being in a flying machine suspended above the earth.

It only took a few years for the architectural studio founded by Roman Delugan and Elke Meissl to leap over the Olympus of international notoriety, winning a series of important competitions. Currently they are working on projects all over Europe including a museum for Porsche in Stuttgart, a cinema museum in Amsterdam, and the new campus for the University of Technology in Vienna.

They live in a penthouse apartment, in the center of Vienna, created by adding a story to a sixties vintage office building. Built following Delugan & Meissl's plans, the penthouse is set back from the façade of the building. It is not quite visible from the street, but it cannot go unnoticed when viewed from an appropriate distance. With its aerodynamic shapes and aluminum and glass surfaces that reflect variations in the sky, it calls to mind a spaceship, from a technologically and aesthetically advanced civilization, graciously positioned on a city rooftop; the name given to the residence, *Ray 1*, also brings to mind a spacecraft.

With the sole exception of the bedrooms and bathrooms, no partitions interrupt the fluidity of a path that winds through the internal space; continuity with the exterior is resolved by a game with the glass walls that shape the apartment's terraces.

Taking the precepts of an illustrious fellow citizen, Adolf Loos (one of the fathers of modern architecture and author of the famous essay *Ornament and Crime*), to the extreme, not only is every decorative element banished from the decor but (apart from a few chairs and tables) all the

Above: The central area of the lower floor is characterized by the aerodynamic multiuse counter that defines the kitchen area and by the custom-made leather sofa set in the wall. The large window makes the divide with the outside seem impalpable, while the continuity of the internal spaces is emphasized by the uninterrupted wood flooring.

Right: A niche used as an office is separated from the living area by layers of glass shelving suspended from the ceiling and by a curtain which is a work by Viennese artist Erwin Bohatsch. Also seen are a few elements belonging to the history of design: a *Lounge Chair* by Charles and Ray Eames and a *Bracket* lamp by Archille Castiglioni.

furniture has been absorbed by the architecture. In their place are sculpted volumes and intersecting surfaces that are, more often than not, multifunctional. All this brings to life a fascinating new kind of domestic landscape. The value of this essential, elemental architecture is enhanced, rendered more precious, by the contrasting materials and colors, graphic-design-inspired fittings, and a mixture of natural and artificial lighting.

Beyond the glass door of the relaxing area, a sailing boat floats on a thin veil of water that marks the edge of one of the terraces; it is only a model, but with the rooftops of Vienna as a backdrop, it seems like a mirage. A house of the future, suspended between the sky and the city, must be a place to dream.

Opposite: Each wall is designed to contain or enclose. These creations—the shelving in the foreground and the wardrobes to the side, whose shaped doors recall Lucio Fontana's *slashes*—are examples of three dimensional graphic design. The chairs are classic pieces by Henry Bertoia.

Above: The kitchen area occupies a different level in the open space, emphasized by the play of volumes between the wooden platform and the white multiuse counter.

Left and opposite: The kitchen area is composed of transparent, white, and wooden surfaces. The storage units and work surfaces interrupt the continuity of the large windows that face the main terrace.

Above and opposite: The terrace, seen from inside and outside. The wooden flooring, with a different finish, extends to the outside and accommodates a tuft of marsh vegetation. The surface stops at the edge of a basin with a model sailboat—creating an evocative image that uses the city rooftops as a backdrop.

Overleaf: The integration of the furnishings with the architecture, the absence of partitions or opaque closures, and the layout of this penthouse apartment all combine to the create a fluid space.

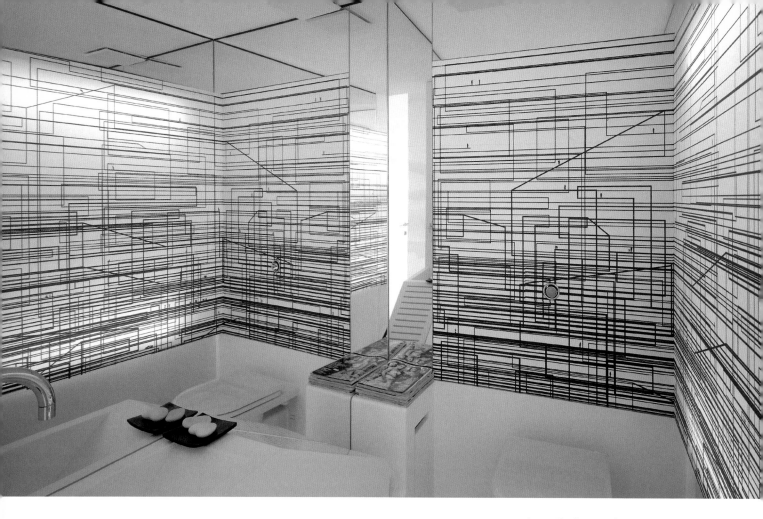

Above: The lines on the bathroom walls are reminiscent of Paul Klee's drawings in China ink. The bathroom and bedrooms are the only rooms enclosed on four sides.

Right and overleaf: Two views of the bedroom, which also has a bathtub and a sink. The custom-made bed—like the entire house—seems to detach itself from the earth and rise toward the Viennese sky, visible through the large windshield of *Ray I*.

OPEN-AIR INTERIOR
—*Parma*

Right: Built during the second half of the eighteenth century, this large hayloft has been converted into a summer residence.

Overleaf: Climbing plants ascend the main façade of the structure and work their way into the interior of the second floor, which lacks closures or fixtures that separate the inside from the outside. The cast iron pieces of garden furniture are original English pieces from the second half of the nineteenth century, forged by the historic factory of Colbrookdale.

Fontanellato, near Parma in the heart of Italy's Emilian countryside, is the birth town of the great sixteenth-century painter Parmigianino. It is also the location of a vast agricultural estate chosen by Franco Maria Ricci as a summer residence and headquarters for the foundation that carries his name.

The restoration work on a villa and its surrounding structures, which date back to the eighteenth century, was done over the course of thirty years and reflects the personality of the owner. A publisher of elegant art books, and an expert on applied arts and architecture, Franco Maria Ricci has always harbored a particular passion for early nineteenth-century England. The work at Fontanellato draws inspiration from this era of picturesque styles and romantic gardens. Though restoration sought to maintain the rural character of structures, the objective of the renovation was not to make a faithful reconstruction of the original buildings.

The interior of the main villa was converted to house a museum and the library of the FMR foundation. An enormous adjoining hayloft, supported by characteristic pillars of brick, was shaped into Franco Maria Ricci's summer residence. In order to preserve the original character of the structure (which was open on the sides to assist the natural drying process of the hay) all types of closures, even glass closures, were reduced to a minimum. The living room, which occupies the entire upper level of the hayloft, has the appearance of a covered terrace and is completely immersed in the smells and sounds of the countryside. Though the old trussed

Above: A view of the yard surrounding the hayloft, paved with terracotta.

Opposite: From the second floor terrace/living room one can catch a glimpse of hidden corners of the residence, simply furnished spaces perfect for reading and relaxing.

Overleaf: Supported by brick pillars and wooden trusses, the roof of the old hayloft is the only thing that protects the living room from the elements.

roof continues to provide excellent protection from the summer heat and rain, the space is completely exposed to the wind and passing birds. Climbing plants wind around the brick pillars that support that roof and enter inside to mingle with the plants kept in earthenware pots along the edges of the terrace space. Everything is perfectly integrated with the surrounding countryside, once open farmland which over time has become increasingly wooded.

After a long career in publishing Franco Maria Ricci has focused his enthusiasm and imagination on the outdoors. Working with the municipality of Fontanellato, his goal is to transform his estate into an English style park that will be open to the public. This park will also include a bamboo garden (another of the owner's passions). Visitors will be able to admire his library amassed over the course of a lifetime, walk among nature, and perhaps sit down to taste the local cuisine.

Opposite and right: In the center of the terrace/living room is a long masonry dining table with a Sardinian marble top and two lamps designed by Marianna Gagliardi.

Overleaf, left: Berber mats woven with straw and wool are spread on the terracotta floor. Surrounding the large table is an ensemble of cane furniture. A ceramic lamp in the shape of a pine cone, created in a local artisan workshop, sits among the vases on the back wall.

Overleaf, right: A corner of the living room. The wooden chair was made in India and dates back to the English colonial period.

127

Right: The kitchen area, also located under the truss roof of the hayloft, is open to the elements. The fixed furnishings were created using bricks from the original building. The countertops are Sardinian granite slabs.

Overleaf: The rustic furnishings include a chest of drawers with a stone top.

Above and opposite: Though nature may be allowed to come into direct contact with the living spaces on the second floor of the structure, it is kept out of the ground floor. The restructured space, with iron framed windows and doors, is like a white crypt. Numerous carpets spread on the terracotta floor confer a vague Oriental atmosphere to the room. The furniture includes low black lacquered bookcases, a garden table, and a few antique pieces, among which are two episcopal busts placed to watch over the entrance.

POSTMODERN VERNACULAR
—*Buggiano*

Right: In the living room, the stone fireplace is flanked by cabinets made with laminates by Abet. The armchair is by Kita for Cassina and the vases are pieces from the *100% Make Up* series coordinated by Alessandro Mendini. The miniature prototype armchair sitting on the custom-made glass table is also Alessandro Mendini. The two blue sofas are by Francesco Binfarè for Edra.

For Tuscan architect Massimo Mariani redesigning a house requires organizing and combining pre-existing and new volumes. His work, according to noted Italian architecture critic Lara-Vinca Masini, often entails "transforming into architecture what was previously a banal construction immersed in an anonymous landscape." But in this case Mariani's project is located in the hills of Montecatini Terme, an area of exquisite natural beauty that is protected by the government of Italy, an area that certainly cannot be considered ordinary.

Mariani's conversion of a nineteenth-century farmhouse into a contemporary residence maintains the structure and austerity of the original building. Missing sections of the original walls were restored in order to bring back the simple and elegant character of the interiors. The renovation also took the surrounding landscape into account. A grassy terrace with a view of hilly countryside was constructed in front of the main façade of the house.

While the exterior remains that of a typical Tuscan farmhouse the interior, with its playful colored volumes and double height spaces, has a postmodern flavor. The house has two floors; the entrance area accentuates the two level divide and is the center of the house. A teak stairway, that wraps around a red chimney-like architectural element, leads to the sleeping area. Yellow built-in cupboards in the kitchen walls contrast with the blue furnishings in the bathroom. The whole surpasses stylistic categories and becomes a game of colors.

Left: A wooden staircase on the left leads to the second floor. The chair framed by the window is a reproduction of Mackintosh's *Willow* chair. The newly added grassy terrace is just visible through the window.

Opposite: The chair and table on the second floor landing are re-editions from the *Blue-Red* series by Gerrit Rietveld.

Above: The teak stairs that wrap around the red volume lead to the bedrooms. The painting on the wall on the right is by Alessandro Mariani.
Left: The red chimney-like structure contains a bathroom.
Opposite: The kitchen is visible through the doorway on the right.

Left, above: Doorways in the walk-in wardrobe lead to the bedroom (on the right) and the bathroom (on the left). Soft colored laminate panels and beech wood give the space a warm and welcoming atmosphere. Customized with a plate painted by Massimo Mariani, the ceiling light is by Castiglioni for Flos.

Left, below: The surfaces of the fixtures in the master bathroom are covered with blue laminate; the tiles on the walls and floor are made of recomposed marble. The shower is outfitted with blue *Vetricolor* tiles by Bisazze.

Opposite: The custom-made kitchen furnishings also make use of laminated panels. The *Italcom* chairs are made of beech wood. The painting on the wall on the right is by Massimo Mariani.

DOMESTIC BRUTALISM
—*Carrara*

Right: Every corner Patty Nicoli's home, created inside an eighteenth-century structure, has examples of her work. This image shows the living room, which faces the garden where the owner collects the blocks of marble that will become sculptures.

Rich in historic value and known throughout the world, the marble quarries that lie in the mountains behind the city of Carrara are treasured by the great masters who work the stone. In the center of Carrara, not far from the Calocara quarry, a small nineteenth-century palazzo is home to the Nicoli family. Next door, in front of a huge garden that serves as a storage area for blocks of marble and works in progress, is an old sculpture workshop that has belonged to the family since the end of the eighteenth century. Six generations of talented artisans have created magnificent works commissioned by famous artists and displayed in the greatest museums of the world, from the Vatican to New York. But the Nicoli family is not only a family of marble artisans, they are also a family of artists and patrons of the arts. For years the house hosted the sculptor Arturo Martini, and today it continues to be a guesthouse for artists.

A short distance away, in an old cottage, Patty Nicoli (sculptor Carlo Nicoli's sister) created an enchanting workshop that has become her home. It is here that the sculptress shapes choice material to create her own works of art. "I was born into marble and I could not do without it," she confesses. Patty Nicoli's home is made of brutally exposed building materials.

The house is spread over two floors. The original appearance of the ground floor of the structure, which was used for storage in the seventeenth century, has been left intact. For example a soaring brickwork arch in the living room remains exposed. A recently added iron staircase leads to an

Right: An iron staircase, which has become an informal bookshelf, leads to the elevated platform where a bedroom and bathroom are located.

Overleaf, left: A few of Patty Nicoli's sculptures rest on a wooden shipping crate.

Overleaf, right: The seventeenth-century storage cellar turned modern home integrates exposed brickwork and flooring made with seven different types of Carrara marble.

Opposite: The bathroom is located upstairs. Even here the floor is made of marble. The bathtub is inserted into the top of an arched window.

Above: The wood-floored bedroom, also located upstairs, is illuminated and ventilated by a semicircular window. The small space is used efficiently; a writing desk is placed under an old arch in the wall.

Overleaf: In the kitchen coarse exposed brick walls are juxtaposed with smooth marble countertops, sinks, and flooring. Hanging copper pots and pans provide a decorative furnishing motif.

elevated platform (the second floor) which is where the bedroom is located.

A few of the windows are characterized by arcs of multicolored fans with yellow, blue, and fuchsia colored glass. The prismatic light that filters through this creates marvelous contrasts with the neutral earth tones, and the gray and white marble, that dominate the interior. In addition to sculptures in the famous pure white Carrara marble, the interior contains marble topped tables, sinks, and flooring realized with at least seven different types of veined local marble. The stone, brick, terracotta, and wood, "poor" materials par excellence, find renewed splendor in this rural residence and share the space with the precious local material, Carrara marble. The presence of these two different types of material does not compromise the homogeneity and harmony of these rough, but elegant domestic interiors.

VACATION TEMPLE
—*Minorca*

Right: A patio acts as a buffer between the interior living room and the space outside. The *Astrolabio* table and the *Abanica* chairs are from the Solaria collection designed by Oscar Tusquets for Aleph. The silverware is also by Tusquets for Officina Alessi.

Boasting marvelous small coves and an emerald colored sea, Minorca, the lesser known of Spain's Balearic Islands, has everything to recommend it: 125 miles of beach interspersed with magnificent coves, some only reachable on foot, a wonderful uncontaminated sea, and a peace and tranquillity unknown elsewhere. The people of the island knew how to preserve their traditional ways of life and local customs, without creating a chaotic urban increase or attracting mass tourism. Perhaps this is the reason a young lawyer decided to have his house built here. To escape the urban chaos of an increasingly congested Barcelona, he asked the architects Oscar Tusquets and Carlos Diaz to design a reasonably sized and priced villa. What was originally intended as a holiday home, immersed in greenery and facing the sea, became a daily residence.

The villa has only one floor and its design has a formal simplicity, being based on the simplest and purest shape that exists— the square. The rooms, similarly sized to one another, allow for constant encounters between external and internal space. Some of the porches can be transformed into interior spaces, thanks to a series of tall shutters, resulting in a complex of closed and open spaces that flow from one to the other. Each space is filled with light that filters through pergolas, transparent shelving, and shutters painted a wonderful shade of turquoise. Various shades of blue frame the entire residence. The blue detailing and furnishings are set off by the white walls which increase the luminosity of the house. Though the style of the architecture call to mind many

Right: The living room is connected to the patio. The rug incorporated in the *Ali Baba* sofa was designed by Oscar Tusquets and produced by Casas. The cast iron column functions both as a structural and decorative element.

of the rural constructions in the area, the gables, pilasters, and bas-reliefs that decorate the façade, are reminiscent of the neoclassical style of architecture imported by the English. The house is a significant contribution to the creation of a new Mediterranean style, a short hop from the sea.

Left: The *Ali Baba* sofa, stackable *Garcela* tables for Aleph and the porcelain tea set for Folies/Driade were all designed by Oscar Tusquets. The two cane and steel armchairs were designed by Pete Sans and produced by b.d Ediciònes de Diseño. The *Mesa Tarantina* console table (in the foreground on the right) and the *T.M.M.* floor lamp (on the left) designed by Miguel Milà are both produced by Santa & Cole.

Overleaf, left: Transparent shelving allows a view of a cove to be enjoyed. The crystal glasses and the porcelain tea set were designed by Tusquets for Follies/Driade.

Overleaf, right: The kitchen table is *Sube y baja* by Robert Heritage and Roger Webb for Disform, the *Potro* chairs are by Oscar Tusquets for Carlos Jané Camacho. The dish-covers on the bottom right are another design by Tusquets for Follies/Driade.

Previous pages, left: The *Joker* sofa is by Alberto Llevore and Jorge Pensi for Perobell, the *Garcela* tables are by Tusquets for Aleph and the *Luna* rug for b.d Ediciònes de Diseño.

Previous pages, right: The *Astrolabio* table, *Luna* rug and *Pineta* sofa by Oscar Tusquets.

Left: The bathroom and bedroom are a single space. The *Mirac* coat stand, next to the bed covered with a fabric by Gaston y Daniela, is by Massaia-Tremolada for Mobles 114. The armchair was modeled by Jorge Pensi for Perobell. The bathtub, encased in gray marble, faces the solarium-terrace; the iron plant on the shelf is from the *Plantarium* series designed by Guillem Bonet and Alicia Nuñez for Santa & Cole.

Right: In front of the bed is a small veranda with a fan-shaped aperture that overlooks the sea. The sycamore bureau on the crystal table was designed and produced by Jaume Tresserra.

Overleaf: The south face of the villa; the patio that acts as an extension of the living room; a second patio can be seen on the left below the gabled façade.

THE ARCHITECTURE FACTORY
—*Florence*

Above: Claudio Nardi's home and office in a refurbished industrial building is located in the center of Florence.
Right: A stairway between a living space and a conference area leads to offices.
Overleaf: The large painting resting on the floor is by Arnold Mario Dallò. The sofa, armchair and floor lamp are from the sixties, while the small table (from the fifties) is openly inspired by an Alvar Aalto design.

Situated in the heart of Florence, Claudio Nardi's office (and at times his home) occupies a structure that shows its history as an industrial building. Built during the thirties, the building was incorporated into what was once the largest laundry in the city of Florence immediately after the World War II. Subsequently it became the site of various artisans' workshops. Claudio Nardi moved his architectural practice to this space in the eighties.

The latest restoration work was done in 2004. Original structural elements were left visible, keeping the industrial character of the complex. Many of the lofty spaces were maintained, others were converted to intermediate height rooms. The original reinforced concrete trusses, which have been inspected and cleaned, were considered to be technologically advanced when they were erected. The choice of almost invisible light fixtures accentuates the spare decor. Paintings are hung with bare wire, or rest on the floor, creating a provisional atmosphere.

Opposite: The living room of the office space as seen from the meeting room. The partitions, thinly framed panes of glass, are designed to make them less obtrusive and to create the impression that the area is one continuous space.
Above: Hanging under a concrete truss is *Elaborations* by Giacomo Costa.
Overleaf, left: A detail of Costa's imaginary city.
Overleaf, right: The double height space seen from above. Work spaces for Nicoli's architecture studio occupy the upper level.

There are no partitions to define borders between private areas and working areas; the divisions created by walls, balconies, and glass doors seem to be ephemeral. The professional spaces take on the welcoming quality of the residential space. Only simple, essential materials are used: polished steel, glass, concrete, wood, and drywall. Favoring black, white, and tones of gray, the "color" palette of the space is quite elegant. The furnishings and decorative objects, despite being slightly vintage in style, are either contemporary pieces, custom-made, or acquired from flea markets. Works by artists (such as Giacomo Costa, Sherry Mills and Arnold Mario Dallò), friends, and from Sergio Tossi's nearby contemporary art gallery fill the former commercial laundry. The spaces intermingle, unite and transform each room into a metropolitan blend not often found in the Renaissance city.

Opposite: View of the residential area. The iron staircase leads to the floor above where the bedrooms are located.

Right: Reverse angle of the living area. Behind the curtain in the background on the right is a sauna.

Overleaf: Overall view of the living area. The image of a chain on the left is by Sherry Mills.

Left, top: The large-scale leather sofa is custom-made.

Left, bottom: A metal storage unit marks the entrance to the kitchen.

Opposite: The iron staircase stands between the dining area and the kitchen.

Overleaf, left: Old photographs hung from transparent wires become decorative features.

Overleaf, right: The sleek iron staircase that leads to the upper floors of the residence.

Second overleaf, left: On the second floor a bedroom (through the doorway) and a bathroom (on the left) can be found.

Second overleaf, right: The bedroom on the top floor. The design displayed in the niche headboard is suggestive of barcodes. On the right the structural truss can be seen, screened by a *brise soleil*.

DOLCE & GABBANA

WAREHOUSES
OF DESIGN
—*Amsterdam*

Opposite: The building, which overlooks a canal, was once used to store grain. All the furnishings opposite the entrance are of Dutch origin. The rug is from the twenties, the small table from the forties, and the mahogany and leather armchair was produced and designed by Ulf Moritz in collaboration with the Binnenhuis furnishing center. The floor lamp is by *Xavier Mariscal* for b.d Ediciònes de Diseño.

Buildable land is scarce in the city of Amsterdam; houses grow upward and floor plans squeeze economically sized rooms into as little space as possible. A full-floor apartment is a rarity; those that do exist are considered very extravagant. After a long search, Yvonne Hustl found an old building, formerly used to store grain, to renovate and convert into her home. The structure faces a canal and is typically Dutch, built with small dark bricks. It is in a complex that stands along the edge of Prinseneiland, one of three islets (with Bickerseiland and Realeneiland) where boats are taken to be repaired.

Yvonne Hustl chose not to disturb the original structure to maintain the existing atmosphere of the space, but she did not renounce contemporary comforts. The result of her renovation is a space that is halfway between the openness of a loft and the intimacy of local traditional houses. Hustl's design solution entailed doing away with internal partitions in half the available space, to create a large living area, and subdividing the remaining available space into rooms typically found in a classic house—bathrooms and bedrooms. Quite a bit of space is used, and quite a bit of space is left empty.

The residence has not lost its historic character. The exterior of the building still has a warehouse-like appearance, and the interior, with its refurbished wooden support beams and concrete floors, is clean but industrial looking. The large open rooms have been carefully decorated by Hustl. Each piece of furnishing speaks of her refined taste and passion for matching styles and materials. Classic objects like Gerrit Rietveld's *Zig-Zag Chair* sit next to one-of-a-kind pieces designed for the owner of the house.

The surfaces and materials reveal a feminine touch. The coloring of the walls, mosaic tiles in the bathroom, and pressed fabric curtains, all soften the clear-cut character of this former warehouse space. Hustl has masterfully inserted the polished and comfortable spaces of a private home into this unusually large and luminous space near a shipyard in the Dutch capital.

Above: The dining area is furnished with a table inspired by the Shaker tradition and produced by Edizioni De Padova; the *Suspiral* chairs are by Luigi Serafini for Sawaya and Moroni. The candelabra is by David Palterer for Alterego. A large painting by the Greek artist Irini Scocos stands against the wall.

Opposite: In the sitting room there is a conversation corner with a crystal table on wheels by Gae Aulenti for Fontana Arte; on the table is a vase by Borek Sipek. The sofa bed is an Eileen Gray design, *Day Bed*, produced by Vereingte Werkstätten. A work by Riklina can be seen on the wooden

pillar on the right. The carpet was designed by Daniela Puppa for Sisa; the *Elba* armchairs are by Franco Raggi for Cappellini International Interiors and the *Traccia* table by Meret Oppenheim for Simon International. On the background walls (treated with a sponge-painted effect) the

fake pillars are in bas-relief. The green applique is from the Khoybucky series by Elin Raaberg Nielsen for Vistosi.

Previous pages, left: A corner of the living room has an umbrella artwork by Amanda Palmer; a small *Aprilo* console table with *Cicindela* candlesticks, all by Alessandro Mendini and Bruno Gregori for Zabro.

Previous pages, right: The armchair was designed by Mallet-Stevens in 1928 and reproduced by Ecart International. The *AB* lamp in the corner is by Paolo Deganello for Ycami Collection. The curtain system is inspired by a classic example seen in the Villa Borromeo of Isolabella: it has two side vertical poles that a luxurious drape travels up and down.

Opposite: The vase of red tulips on the wooden dining table gives a Dutch feel. The chandelier is a Yayaho model by Ingo Maurer.

Right: At the entrance the *Les grands trans-Parents* mirror is produced by Simon International and inspired by Man Ray. The console table and *Aprilo* table are by Alessandro Mendini and Bruno Gregori for Zabro. On the right is glassware by Borek Sipek. The *Faretra* lamp on the ceiling was designed by De Pas, D'Urbino, Lomazzi for Artemide. The curved oxidized copper wall stands between the entry and the bathroom. The bathroom floor is lavagna stone, the lamp is a classic Bauhaus piece designed by Marianne Brandt and the "Zig-zag" chair is an artisan version of the original by Rietveld.

BETWEEN SPLENDOR AND DAILY LIFE
—*Rome*

Right: Eighteenth-century views of Rome hang in the entry hall. The furnishing is a combination of original and custom-made pieces that revive and transform decorative baroque motifs—for example the sofa, with its mixtilinear profile, and the burnished-brass floor lamp with its serpent-like design.

Given the canvas of a palace that was once the residence of cardinals in the heart of papal Rome, what kind of domestic landscape can be created beneath its coffered-ceilings? Two architects from Turin, Lorenzo Prando and Riccardo Rosso, were asked to adapt this remarkable space into a residence suited for both public occasions and everyday life. They reintroduced, in contemporary terms, two ways of understanding the decoration of interiors characteristic of the baroque period: the artisan virtuosity of the individual pieces of furniture, and their arrangement within each room according to a studied scheme solids and voids, and color. References to the past, beyond the contrast of antique objects and those that are custom-made (the majority), is entirely conceptual. The shapes that breath life into these new settings, and the selection materials and colors, do not seek to resemble the historic models that inspired them. If anything they betray a certain affinity with the work of some great modern interpreters of the decorative baroque tradition, like the eclectic Mexican aesthete and decorator Carlos de Beistegui, who was acclaimed on the international scene and valued by leading exponents of the rationalist culture like Le Corbusier.

All the elements that characterize Lorenzo Prando and Riccardo Rosso's restyling are present in the entrance vestibule; starting with the juxtaposition of antique and custom-made pieces of furniture and the aggressive use of color that gives the space a theatrical feel (further accentuated here by the large velvet curtain hanging in front of

Above and opposite: The sofas form an almost complete circuit along the walls of the entry hall. Their wooden frames are lacquered with tempera and the covers are velvet and damask. The floors in the entry hall and living room are paved with handcrafted terracotta; the design of the tiles in each room has a different geometry.

Overleaf: Two large custom-made sofas define the central space of the room. The imposing golden-framed baroque mirror reflects the silk curtained windows to each side. The contemporary console table and iron fireplace screen act as counterpoints to the old hearth and the large canvas depicting the Sacrifice of Isaac.

the door). All of the rooms have an ostentatious, but "playful" atmosphere; though this aspect is perhaps less accentuated in the rooms used for entertaining, it can still be seen in the repetition, always in different forms. One example of this playfulness is the serpent, a classic motif, that accompanies the drapes, defines the baroque mirror, the outline of the sofas, and folds down the metal of the fireplace screen in living room. On the other hand, immodest playfulness is the central theme of the more private rooms, with furniture made from laminated plastic panels and *bois de rose*, and progressively dominates the ordinary signs of everyday life (from the modular wardrobe to the bedroom television) inside the same monument. Finally, it triumphs in the master bathroom, decorated with marble slabs that seem like cartoon clouds: an amusing homage to the Bernini fountains and to "deus ex machina" of the late-Renaissance theater.

Second overleaf, left: Custom-made cabinets have been placed in opposite corners of the dining room. They are characterized by the variety of materials used: metal uprights, laminate sides, mirror and wooden panels with various types of veneers.

Second overleaf, right: In the dining room a glass tabletop is supported by a system of straight and curved legs—sandblasted stainless-steel and copper respectively—and surrounded by original Louis XIV-style chairs. The Murano glass chandelier dates to the eighteenth century.

Previous pages, left: A more intimate living room houses a desk inspired by the decorative inventions of Carlos de Beistegui, finished in laminated plastic and rosewood. On the left stands an *Aggregato* floor lamp by Artemide (designed by Enzo Mari and Giancarlo Fassina).

Previous pages, right: A dialogue is woven between the nineteenth-century wall decorations, Venetian-style floor motifs, and the patterns of the fabric that covers the soft furnishings.

Above: The sofa bed is designed by Prando and Rosso is juxtaposed along one wall of the boudoir.

Opposite: The striking wardrobe is covered in the same materials as the writing desk; the panels can be detached from the doors to reveal mirrors. The small black obelisks that crown the piece create a dialogue with the coffered ceiling.

Opposite and above: In the
bathroom, the patterns of
the fittings and wood plank
flooring play with the outlines
of wavy cuts of marble
inspired by Bernini's fountains.
The fluorescent lamps that
run along the edge of the
mirror are reminiscent of old
barbershop poles.

Opposite: Wood is the main feature of the bedroom with its patterned floor and the headboard (which is also a storage unit) of the bed. The bed itself rests on an iron structure. The large canvas facing the bed dates from the eighteenth century.

Right: A pleasing game of overlapping "broken" mirrors plays out on the laminate and natural wood paneled wardrobe.

Overleaf, left: The drapes and colors in the entrance hall reflect those in the eighteenth-century canvas hung above the console table, and bring them to life in three dimensions. The restoration has given a theatrical quality to all the rooms in the palace, linking a respect for history with a courageous experimentation of forms and materials.

Overleaf, right: The warm light of the Roman afternoons heightens the chromatic interplay between the walls, curtains, and furnishing elements, revealed by this view from the sitting room, which is typical of baroque interiors.

CONTEMPORARY ECLECTIC
—*St. Gallen*

Right: In the dining area, a *Polidoro* table by Adolfo Natalini for Driade Antologia is coupled with *Costes* chairs by Philippe Starck for Aleph.
Overleaf: View of the open space that contains the living and dining areas.

The ivy covered Villa Rosenhof on the hills of St. Gallen resembles an English country house, not the Swiss mountain chalets typical of the area. Built by the architect Julius Kunkler in 1904, the villa's distinctive asymmetrical structure, references to late neo-Gothic style, and the presence of bay windows, *altanas* (Venetian-style roof terraces), verandas, terraces, stone loggias and façades with exposed beams are all throwbacks to English houses from the start of the century. The house once accommodated an entire patriarchal family. Architect Peter Frischknecht's renovation plan for the villa creates a structure more adapted to modern, nuclear families.

Though the resorations sought to preserve as much as possible of the original structure of the building, Frischknecht began his remodeling by knocking down the main staircase and closing off the ground floor space to create his apartment. The interior, like the exterior, is united by a single decorative element from which the name of the

Above: A nook in the living room opens onto a small terrace and the garden.

Opposite: The *Lucas* chairs by Oscar Tusquets for Aleph are next to a small *Vicieuse* table by Philippe Starck. The *Louis I* chandelier is by Borek Sipek.

Overleaf, left: The *Affusoalato* table, *Stammgast* chair and *Sapienzale* bookshelf in the study were all designed by Adolfo Natalini for Periplo. The *Paramount* armchairs are also by Philippe Starck for Aleph.

Overleaf, right: The bedroom also overlooks the garden. The Franz Joseph four-poster bed is by Antonia Astori for Aleph. The *Astrolabio* table in the foreground is by Oscar Tusquets for Aleph.

villa itself derives: the rose. Made following line drawings by Kunkler, the rose is depicted in different materials—from wrought iron to glass, iron to oil and canvas—and adorns and embellishes the gates, window gratings, the glass doors or walls of the internal rooms, and the wrought-iron structures that support the entrance's barrel vault. The residence is not only distinguished by the elegance of the architectural and decorative elements but also by the furnishings, which are seldom period pieces and favor contemporary selections gathered in an eclectic manner. The owner chose works by Philippe Starck (who often links traditional forms with contemporary elements and well-known materials in daring guises) to emphasize and strengthen the coherence of his hybrid house. There is a reassuring presence of wood in the dining room; Adolfo Natalini's Polidoro table is paired with the French designer's Costes chairs. Only the bathroom maintains the usual fittings and original large windows, and has just one design object: Borek Sipek's

Helena chair. Given the venerable exterior of Villa Rosenhof the eclectic atmosphere of this contemporary interior is an unexpected find.

Opposite: The bathroom has kept the original fixtures and detailed glass door and windows.

Right: Another *Astrolabio* table by Oscar Tusquets is accompanied by two cane armchairs, *Liba* and *Prorok*, by Borek Sipek for Driade Antologia.

Right, below: There is a small balcony facing the garden off the main living room.

Overleaf: The entrance to the villa seen from two different angles.

MODERNITY AND SIGNS OF THE TIMES
—*London*

Right: The dining room table is an old jewelry workbench. The unusual use and juxtaposition of work-furniture, antique pieces, and ethnic or designer objects is the underlying theme for the furnishing of this interior renovated by Jean-François Delsalle for the designer Yvonne Sporre.

Creating unconventional new living spaces that make bold references to the design styles of past generations is a trend that became popular when postmodern styles of furnishing, and its breed of retro nostalgia, began its decline. This trend, based on fresh and attractive combinations of pieces from different places and traditions, is present in the decor of Yvonne Sporre's English apartment. Located in London—a city that has been a capital of historic eclecticism and that continues to be the main European laboratory for new trends in interior design—the interiors of the apartment reflect the cosmopolitan circumstances that brought its design into being. French architect Jean-François Delsalle has created interiors for many trendy Parisian shops and haunts. Sporre, born in Sweden, was an internationally famous model in the seventies who then became a designer at the Italian fashion house Missoni.

The address is an elegant residential street in Shepherd's Bush that, like many other London streets, has seemingly identical rows of terraced houses extending for hundreds of feet. Sometimes, behind the monotonous composition of the façades, strong and unexpected individual personalities are revealed, recognizable in this case by the passion behind the choice of each piece of furniture and their careful arrangement. The renovation implemented by Delsalle is radical: nearly all the pre-existing internal partitions have been demolished, the wooden staircase leading to the mansard has been replaced with a metal ladder, and windows of different shapes and sizes have been placed in

Right: The kitchen and dining area takes up a large corner of the living room and was created by demolishing several internal walls. The technological materials in the kitchen have been combined with wood and the soft forms of objects from the past. The seats originally belonged to different sewing machine models.

the roof. The rooms are spacious, bright, and modern (but not neutral); in fact they are so modern that the architectural elements belonging to the original structure—the bay windows and fireplaces for example—seem like objets trouvés, evidence of the near past. The furnishings hold hints of the remote past: ethnic furniture from the colonial period, an eighteenth-century crystal drop chandelier, neo-Gothic stone fireplaces, and a very unusual assortment of work-related furniture from the end of the nineteenth century. In this residence the capable Delsalle has given coherence and meaning to extremely varied design cues and made associations that appear completely natural.

Previous pages, left: The Italian chandelier in the living room is from the eighteenth century. An aluminum staircase leads to the second floor. The flooring is made of pale oak boards and the walls, treated with a single coat of paint, seem to mediate between the contemporary rigor of the architecture and the references to the past that loom in the furnishings.

Previous pages, right: A colonial armchair and a bed (used here as a table) from the nineteenth century, both from India, are arranged in front of the bay window, which is framed by white velvet curtains. The photographic lamp is of French origin.

Left: One side of the living room is decorated with two stone fireplaces acquired from the London Architectural Salvage and Supply Company (LASSCO). The metal armchair belonged to a German barber shop from the early twentieth century.

231

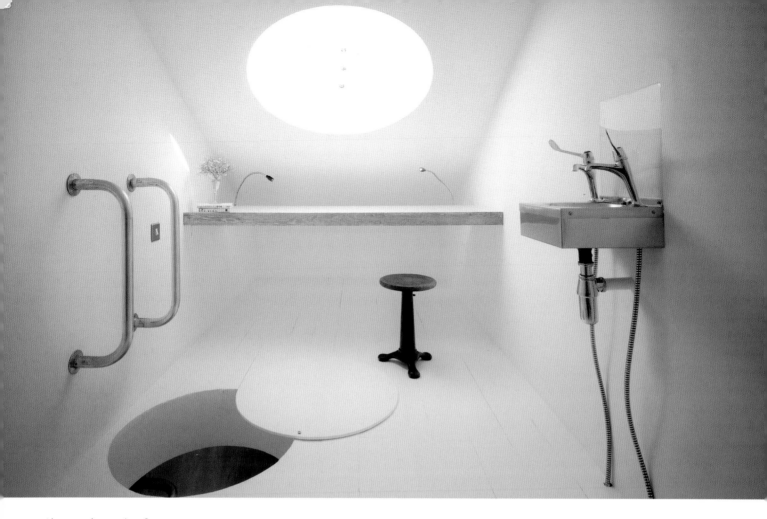

Above and opposite: On
the upper floor, the space is
divided by sliding partitions
that separate or allow the
creation of a continuous space;
when these partitions are
closed the sleeping area is a
small private chamber; a sailor-
style ladder leads through
a trap door to a small attic
bathroom lit by a porthole-
shaped skylight.

Left and opposite: The main bathroom is furnished with wood. The floor is pale oak. The paneling of the wardrobes and the low wall opposite is made of multilayered wood used for boats. The nineteenth-century bathtub, which comes from a Welsh castle, is also made of wood and is used as a shower platform.

Overleaf: This collection of chairs also includes antique curiosities; the armchair with a bullhorn frame is from the Edwardian era, and classics of modern design, like the *Sacco* of Gatti, Paolini and Teodori armchairs by Zanotta. The chests of drawers (overleaf, left) are old pieces of furniture from English pharmacies.

GUNS AND FLOWERS
—*Beijing*

Above: A view of the outside of the loft where Huang Rui lives and works. His home was created inside an unused block of the ex-industrial citadel of Dashanzi, half an hour from the center of Beijing.

Right: The renovation exploits the rationalist structure of the building, designed by German engineers, with the extension of the supported platform and the new wood and metal staircase that contrasts with the pre-existing concrete stairs.

Within the theme of hybrid spaces, the ex-industrial complex "798" in Dashanzi on the outskirts of Beijing is a unique case. Its story begins at the start of the fifties, with solidarity between communist regimes. A military components factory—or rather, a city-factory occupying an area of 150 acres—was created with state-of-the-art criteria designed by technical experts of the German Democratic Republic: a piece of East Berlin transplanted into Mao's Peking. History then took its course. Forty years later the German Democratic Republic disappeared and the People's Republic opened up to the market becoming, in a short period of time, a leader on the global scene not only in the field of economics, but also increasingly in artistic and cultural arenas.

Area "798" can be looked upon as a symbolic site of this second Chinese "revolution." None of the other production units (also identified with numbers: 797, 706, 701 etc.) managed to survive international competition. However, at the turn of the millennium new tenants began to repopulate the old pavilions, attracted by the vastness of the rooms, the sober rational elegance of the architecture and the ridiculously low rents. Painters, musicians, galleries, and creative professionals from all genres, together with cultural institutions such as the Central Academy of Fine Arts in Beijing and the important Tokyo Gallery, established outposts in 798. In the space of three years, the military industry surrendered free reign to artistic experimentation and "Bohemian ways." Today, the factory model has by now changed into an Oriental version of New

Left and opposite: On either side of the central table are two long benches (one of which is made from a tree trunk) that create a backdrop for a display of the artist's works. Among the works on display are Plexiglass Twin Towers on the table and a painting on the wall, inspired by the SARS epidemic that affected China in 2002.

Overleaf, left: The kitchen is located behind a glass-paneled wall, and even here the industrial character of the original building is preserved.

Overleaf, right: One of the artist's works hangs on the left wall—*The 3 Written Works* triptych from 2003.

Opposite and above: An elevated platform is located directly below the large sawtooth-roof windows and accommodates a studio and bedroom. After having launched the "Dashanzi Art District" with shows and publications, Huang Rui is now working on another ambitious project: a new area to accommodate the artistic community of Dashanzi, which is currently under threat by massive increases in prices—a product of Dashanzi's success and the ongoing invasion of fashion shops and restaurants.

York's SoHo, filling up with workshops, bookshops, fashionable bars and clubs, a rich calendar of exhibitions, fashion shows, and performances, in other words, the "coolest" place in all of Beijing.

Huang Rui is one of the artisans of the Dashanzi rebirth and the man who has done the most to help it gain worldwide recognition with Reconstruction 798 (an event-exhibition in 2003), publications, and the establishment of the Dashanzi International Art Festival in 2004. In his loft, a pavilion in sector 798, the ingredients of the ex-industrial district's past and present are fused with surprising harmony. The furniture harmonizes with the Bauhaus style of the original structure or converses with it by introducing natural elements (the large bench made from a sawn tree trunk in the middle of the residence) and light touches of the East. All around the residence the artist's paintings and installations comment, with "pop" irony, on the paradox of contemporary China, between communism and economic boom.

VINTAGE MINIMALISM
—*Florence*

Immersed in one of the most extraordinary views in the world, this Florentine penthouse built in the sixties was conceived as a single large terrace. Architect Pietro Giorgieri's private residence is located on top of a building erected at the beginning of the twentieth century. The sliding glass doors that define the boundaries of one side of the apartment offer breathtaking views of the historic center and the surrounding countryside. This vista is a backdrop for the living area. When the doors are open this backdrop becomes a living scene; breezes and the golden light of spring and autumn enter the interiors that wind without interruption from the living room, to the dining room and kitchen.

Faced with the powerful impact of this view, loaded with history and culture, the selection of furnishings is intentionally "different": contemporary, basic, and minimalist. The furnishings are designed in harmony with the architectural structure. The most private rooms—bedrooms and bathrooms—are small and "hidden" by a sliding walls of teak. The entire apartment plays on the relationship between this material, which also covers the floor and gives body to the custom-made furniture storage units, and two other types of finishing: the night blue plaster of the volume, situated in the center of the house, that encloses the condominium staircase and accommodates cabinets on its exterior, and the white *scagliola* on all of the other walls, including the wall on one side of the living room that incorporates a fireplace and bookshelf.

The designer and owner of the house chose accessories—lamps, chairs, small tables—that express his particular predilection for industrial design from the period spanning the end of the forties to the beginning of the sixties. This was a very rich period in industrial design characterized by experimental of forms, colors, and technical assembly. Gems like Charles and Ray Eames's small *DAR* armchair in fiberglass and wire, rare and custom-built pieces like the standard lamp made of painted wooden rings designed by a young Paolo Portoghesi, and anonymous objects collected in second-hand markets while traveling around Europe punctuate the interior. These objects contain stories and charms that do not belong to the contemporary feel of the apartment, or to the profound history that filters through the windows, and introduce the lyrical and emotional dimension of dejà-vu into these spaces suspended between, past and present, inside and outside.

Opposite and above: The living area overlooks Tuscan hills and is sited between two terraces. The room is closed on one side by a wall of bookshelves that flank a fireplace. In the photograph on the opposite page, the table in light colored wood and painted glass is from the fifties and the fiberglass and iron rod armchair is *DAR* by Charles and Ray Eames. In the photograph above, the white Regency sofa is by De Padova. The geometries in the Kilim rug, manufactured in Turkey, interrupt the continuity of the teak floor. The floor lamp in the corner behind the sofa is a prototype by Paolo Portoghesi.

Above: In a small sitting area, next to the dining area, a black Recency sofa commands an excellent view of Florence.
Opposite: White, orange, and black chairs by Charles and Ray Eames surround a round custom-made table. The metal ceiling lamp is a piece of Scandinavian design from the sixties.

Overleaf: Designer lamps (on the floor is *Aoy* by Achille Castiglioni and on the low cabinet is *Wire Lamp* by Verner Panton) and vintage objects collected in various European markets breath life into the domestic landscape. The longhaired rug is of Turkish origin.

Above and opposite: The custom-made tables in the kitchen and dining room, the furniture in the kitchen (also custom-made), and the sliding wall that hides the sleeping area and the bathroom are all made of teak. The kitchen chairs are *Plia* armchairs designed in the seventies by Giancarlo Piretti for Castelli.

Overleaf: The teak furnishings in the bedroom and bathroom form an integral part of the renovation of these spaces done in the sixties. The bedside table lamp dates to the fifties.

THE NEW COLORS OF TRADITION
—*Rome*

Right and overleaf: Views of Ilaria Miani's living room in Rome. The sectional soft furnishings of her "modular sitting room" in acid green and fuchsia velvet are the main feature of the room; this color combination is reflected in the color of the walls and carpet.

Florentine designer Ilaria Miani divides her time between Rome and one of the most stunning areas of Italy, Val d'Orcia, a few kilometers from Siena. Over the course of roughly twenty years she and her husband Giorgio have dedicated themselves to the restoration of old farms. They own five of them and have converted them into ideal vacation homes for refined Italians and travelers from all over the world. The difficulty of finding elegant and functional furniture for these houses was one of the Ilaria's motivations for becoming a designer. She began her adventure in the world of design with her own workshop making frames; over time this workshop transformed itself into a hotbed of ideas for the house and garden. It was the design of her outdoor furniture, inspired by English colonial styles, that first brought her notoriety in Italy and abroad. Today two showrooms, in Rome and Genoa, display a collection of her work that includes upholstered furnishings, four-poster beds, dinner services, and even small kitchen utensils. The style of all of these objects is deliberately unrelated to swings in fashion. The pieces have the authenticity and durability of artisan works; their designer does not pursue the production of series in great numbers. In fact much of the catalog is still produced in the workshops of Tuscan artists.

The materials and styles of workmanship have changed and multiplied over time, from the much-loved solid wood to iron, French-polished furniture, and ceramic pieces. But the original "domestic" inspiration has not changed. This is evident in the family home in Rome which is also a creative laboratory

Above: The *Tripolina* outdoor chairs are now a classic in the Miani catalog; they are well suited for enjoying the terrace that overlooks the rooftops of Trastevere. The small tables are part of the *Tris* series also designed by Ilaria Miani.

Opposite: Even a masonry ledge next to the steps that create the change in level in the center of the sitting room is an occasion to experiment with compositions of objects, forms, and color to create a domestic landscape: a glass vase with violet-stained roses and a set of bowls on a lacquered tray, all in red and orange tones.

and testing ground for Ilaria Miani's products. The house has a terrace that has been enclosed under metal trusses and that is used as a dining room. The space has not been turned into a typical loft with over-sized rooms and bare walls, on the contrary the energy and colors of the objects inundate every corner and clusters of large and small paintings envelop the walls. Nearly all the "pieces"—ornaments or modular sofas—give the impression of furniture that can be disassembled and reassembled in thousands of different ways, according to the occasion, mood, or inspiration of the moment.

Opposite: A composition on the living room table includes geometric iron vases with fresh and dried flowers next to a decorated vase by Tristano di Robilant and a pastel by Mondino (the chocolates stuck to the frame are the artist's invention).

Above: The colors in the living room appear again in this sitting room/study fitted with furniture and complementary pieces signed "IM." The treated solid beech wood chairs can be folded, like the majority of the chairs produced by Ilaria Miani. A practical consideration but also an homage to the English colonial tradition of making easily transportable furniture. A table lamp dedicated to the English sculptress Barbara Hepworth sits on the small table in the background.

Top left: A *secretaire* and folding stool sit next to the lacquered wood *Colonna* floor lamp. A "pop" portrait of Orlano Miani, Ilaria's son, painted by Jacopo Baruchello, sits on the glass console table.
Below left: The iron four-poster bed forms part of the *Classic* collection (*Polonaise* model). The wall behind the bed is covered in paintings, all with different frames.
Opposite: A small two-shelved alder-wood table from the *Octagons* series acts as a bedside table.
Overleaf: The modular wood shelving and dressing table (detail on the right) in the bathroom are inspired by the "What Not," a piece of English furniture used to display ornaments and various objects, in use between the eighteenth and nineteenth centuries. Violet and fuchsia dominate the textiles, while black and white dominate the objects, creating a notable chromatic effect.

Opposite and top right: The kitchen furnishings—the adjustable height light with glass lampshade and the marbletop table that evoke kitchens from a certain era, the uncoordinated appliances, and the presence of contemporary art—reinforce the "lived in" atmosphere that is the stylistic signature of the Miani house.
Bottom right: This outdoor iron and glass table is laid with Miani production tableware and cutlery.

Left: An informal dining
area has been set up on the
small veranda connected by
a staircase to the kitchen and
terrace above.

Overleaf, left: Rolls of
cyclamen colored paper act as
flowers in this composition on
the table in the study which is
also cluttered with trays, paper
holders, and wooden boxes.
The cylindrical vases are made
of black rubber, a material
that has only recently entered
Miani's household range. An
ancient "birds-eye" view of
Rome occupies the back wall.

Overleaf, right: The dining
room is located in a metal
trussed terrace: a sort of
homage to one of the first
industrial areas in Rome, which
was once located outside
the city walls in this part of
Trastevere. The same industrial
theme is evoked by the doors
on the low piece of furniture
that divides the space and the
grates that cover the windows,
reminiscent of those found in
old factories.

BETWEEN HISTORIC
AND CONTEMPORARY
—*Amsterdam*

Opposite: The dialogue between the past and present is the dominant theme of the furnishing arranged by Yvonne Hulst in this seventeenth-century building. Numerous furnishings are original or date back to the restoration work done in the early nineteenth century; for example the Italian garden scenes (work of the seventeenth-century Dutch painter Moucheron) and the Baccarat chandelier from the eighteenth century in the ground floor drawing room. The conference table in the center of the room is by Tobia Scarpa for Molteni. The transparent bust is by Arman and the cases in the foreground, designed by Alan Belcher, are works of contemporary art.

In the heart of Amsterdam, there is a historic residence that overlooks the beautiful Keizersgracht canal that belongs to a private collector of contemporary artworks. The design of the interiors of this residence were created by an important furniture gallery in the city, Yvonne Hulst's Binnenhuis.

The "White House" (the name dates back approximately two centuries before the American residence with the same name came into existence) is listed in all the tourist guides to Amsterdam. It is the work of seventeenth-century architect Philips Vingboons who, together with his brother Justus, was among the first to introduce Holland to elements of the neoclassical style (gables, pilasters, and eaves) within a baroque composition. The White House is an iconic example of this style; its decorative elements and white plaster façade dramatically distinguish the building from those nearby which have Gothic motifs and exposed brick façades.

The interior the building was enlarged in the first half of the nineteenth century.

The magnificent French-style grand staircase dates to this era and, with its winding path and finely crafted wooden handrail, connects the newer volume to the original. The large rooms still have decorative elements from previous centuries, such as wall claddings, detailed ceilings, and chandeliers. These traces of the past stand in contrast to the artworks collected by the owner: paintings, sculptures, installations, for the most part by Dutch artists.

Yvonne Hulst's intervention takes its place amid the heritage of history and contemporary art, and safely draws on a repertoire of "modern classics," particularly those of Italian design. The furniture selected represents a range of styles, from the soft shapes of the upholstered "Chesterfield," echoing the tradition of the nineteenth-century *capitonné*, to the shiny plastic of the *WK* chairs by Verner Panton. These contemporary objects have already stood the test of time, survived fashions, and demonstrated that they are conversant with past styles as well as more

Above: The building faces the Keizersgracht canal and is an example of the architecture of Philips Vingboons from the first half of the seventeenth century.

Above right: In the entrance corridor English neoclassical decorative elements have been adapted to the residential style of building.

Opposite: The monumental staircase, with its magnificent wooden banister, is of French inspiration. It connects the original part of the house to the extension constructed during the first half of the nineteenth century.

Overleaf: Two views of another room belonging to the older part of the "White House." The stucco decorations on the ceiling and the rich wood paneling are original decorative elements, as is the large fireplace clad in ceramic tiles by Jacob de Gheyn. Some sculptures belonging to the owner's collection (on the windowsill in the photograph on the right, ethnic terracotta figures; in the corner in the photograph on the left, *The Three Graces* by Alexander Schabracq) are accompanied by pieces of furniture chosen by Yvonne Hulst, including the low crystal table designed by Gae Aulenti for Fontana Arte.

Second overleaf: In the first floor office, the plaster ceiling and white drapes contrast with the large canvases by Eric van der Grjin, the black leather of the famous chair by Charles and Ray Eames and the plastic of the two Verner Panton chairs. Through the window, the trees in the garden reflect on the glass surfaces of the B&B desk and table-sculpture by Ron Arad. A table lamp designed in 1928 by Charles Martin (still in production) and the floor lamp by Mariano Fortuny complete the furnishing. The sculpture in the corner is a bronze by Kriester.

recent forms of expression. The predilection given to the binary, black and white that also characterizes some of the artworks on display (such as the large "chess board" by Erik van der Grijn hung on the wall of the living room next to the garden) and echoes the contrast between the wood paneling and the existing plasterwork. It can also be interpreted, from a symbolic viewpoint, as the equilibrium of opposites, as the stylistic "code" of the work, or as homage to the architecture of Philips Vingboons and his innovative ideas.

Above and opposite: On the ground floor, the room leading to the garden is an informal sitting room, characterized by two large black and white paintings, the handwoven rug and the "chess board" hung on the wall by of Eric van der Grjin. The smaller artwork on the left is by A.R. Penck. The furnishing is basic: a *Helsinoor* sofa by Lievors and *Pensi*, a metal floor lamp from the fifties, and a small wooden table in the Shaker tradition.

LIVING WITH GAUDÍ
—*Barcelona*

Opposite: The are very few straight lines in Casa Milà. Curving walls characterize the interiors; the floral forms that decorate the walls and doorjambs are accentuated by the lively green paint and blue plasterwork. The flooring is original.

Built between 1905 and 1907, Casa Milà (better known as La Pedrera) was Gaudí's last civil project in Barcelona. Situated near La Rambla on the celebrated Passeig de Gràcia (at number ninety-two), Casa Milà resembles a monumental block of porous stone that curves to follow the contour of the street. Gaudí designed the apartment building keeping faith with the modernist address and exalting his innovative spirit to the full.

There is no symmetry in the Casa Milà; all the floor plans are different from one another. Gaudí was able to create space by eliminating the load-bearing walls and supporting the weight with beams and pillars that allowed him to sculpt the spaces and avoid straight lines. Gaudí decided to use reinforced concrete as the foundation upon which to place fragmented *azulejo* tiles and *pietra viva* (marbleized stucco). These details were then embellished with wrought iron which is used in the doors, balconies, and the structure of the building itself. Another innovative technique is the use of armored glass to construct the transparent flooring of the different balconies in the building.

Today, some of the apartments are privately owned; one of them belongs to the owner of a shop on the ground floor. By law it is not possible to make any structural changes such as knocking down or creating openings in the walls; the layout must remain intact. Yet the owner has managed to personalize his residence by painting the walls with strong colored tones—bright blue and green accentuate the floral and sculptural motifs in this timeless building.

Left: The corridor of the apartment overlooks La Rambla and is used as a storage space for objects and paintings.

Opposite: The interior has been renovated in such a way that it highlights original elements like the floor and the expressionist-style doors.

DOMESTIC ADVENTURES
—*Savona*

Left: A large porthole cut through the dining room wall offers a view onto the living room/office. A few of the furnishings are custom-made (natural maple-wood table and bookshelf with gray aniline treated edges, silk and aluminum chandelier) and a few are designer pieces (the *Arc* lamp by Achille Castiglioni, and an armchair by Poltrona Frau), with the addition of antique pieces (Louis XIII chairs).

A fifteen-story skyscraper built at the end of the thirties near an old watchtower, the symbol of the city (where the humorous and contradictory name "Skyscraper Tower" comes from), dominates Savona's port and skyline marking the start of the Riviera di Ponente. On one of the building's middle floors, Lorenzo Prando and Giorgio Ceretti have renovated an apartment chosen by a shipbuilder as a family home. For structural reasons it was not possible to knock down walls in the apartment; consequently to lessen the severity of the existing layout, the architects focused on color effects, openings giving unusual views from one room to the next, and the recurrence of rounded shapes, both in the design of these openings and in the furnishings. The floor plan is L-shaped and the sequence of living spaces—each one painted a different pastel shade—that occupy the side facing the port has been united by two symmetrical ranks of doorways that give depth to the entire living area. A third row of openings—circular portholes—also perforates the dividing walls, increasing the kaleidoscopic effect of the passages.

Given the location and the client, allusions to the world of the sea and the navy, starting with the portholes, are one of the underlying themes of the decor; but these themes are expressed through poetic evocations and visual suggestions, not through direct references. At the entrance, the twisting shape of the large mirror brings to mind the decorative scrollwork found on old nautical maps. The anodized aluminum and silk chandeliers that hang in the rooms in front of the windows overlooking the port resemble rolled-up sails from vessels of another era, similar to those displayed on the walls and shelves. Gangplanks and hatches are evoked in the shape and use of sheet metal on the dining room tables and in the "green living room," while the upholstered furnishings—also designed by Lorenzo Prando and Giorgio Ceretti—bring to mind the ballrooms of transatlantic liners on the one hand and fishnet meshes on the other, in the texture of the *capitonné*. Clouds and waves shape the surfaces of the main bathroom, in green Gressoney marble—its white streaks resemble white foam on a stormy sea. The custom-made furniture creations, products of fine workmanship, interweave with decorative cultural references, antiques, and carefully selected designer pieces in such a way that everything contributes to veil the space and objects of everyday life in fantasy.

Previous pages, left: In the entrance hallway, the large mirror (with a golden sheet metal frame and natural maple base) is an homage to Parodi, the baroque Ligurian artist. The slate skirting board and doorjambs are also an homage to regional traditions. The multicolored marble Palladian flooring is original (from the late thirties).

Previous pages, right: Facing the opposite direction from the previous photograph: in the foreground are two custom-made pieces of furniture with multilayered birch laminate shelving and natural maple legs. The interior of the sliding door and wardrobe are also in laminate.

Right and opposite: A sequence of portholes pass through the various pastel toned walls of the living area composed of two sitting rooms (green and red), a dining room and living room/office. A twenty-six inch diameter circle is the inspirational shape for many architectural and furniture details. Pairs of natural maple-wood trolleys with painted iron handles and differing functions are positioned along the walls.

Previous pages, left: The doorways that lead through the apartment are framed with red marble shelves. On the left is an armchair designed by George Sowden and manufactured by Memphis. In the background a chest of drawers from the early nineteenth century stands next to a floor lamp by Alessandro Mendini.

Previous pages, right: The expandable dining table, created with techniques, materials, and colors typical of nautical carpentry, is surrounded by Louis XIII chairs. The soft orange furnishings, painted table supports, and vertically adjustable red silk lamp stand out against the light cornflower blue background of the walls.

Opposite: In the red sitting room, the *capitonné* of the custom-made velvet sofas (from a workshop in Turin) and the *Easy Chair* armchairs by Hans J. Wegner revisit fishnet designs in a stylized way. On the left, the *Milo* lamp, reminiscent of an upside-down telescope, by Alessandro Mendini is another allusion to sailing.

Right: In the green sitting room a real telescope stands next to a large sofa—raised to have a better view of the port—covered with *alcantara* and damask. The other padded furnishings are velvet Chareau armchairs. The small table is made of painted sheet metal.

Left: The bathroom is characterized by the contrast between the black Marquinia marble on the floor and the green Gressoney marble used on the walls and the structure that incorporates mirrors and the sinks.

Opposite: In the kitchen, white Carrara marble is used for the multilevel table in the center of the room, the work surface under the window, and the cooking area surface. A custom-made blue glass hood hangs above the latter, from the outside its internal light appears to be a candle. Above the table, surrounded by folding seats designed by Enzo Moretti and manufactured by Zanotta, different types of lamps are assembled to form a single large chandelier. The cabinets (again custom-made) are covered in laminate the same cream color as the walls.

Acknowledgements

The authors would like to thank all the owners and designers of the houses included in this book for allowing our photographers to visit their splendid interiors.

The text of "The Halls of Art" was provided by Quirino Conti and was previously published in the February 2007 issue of *Casamica*.